THE OLYMPICS

MODERN OLYMPICS

HAYDN MIDDLETON

Heinemann Library
Chicago, Illinois

© 2004 Heinemann Library

a division of Reed Elsevier Inc.

Chicago, Illinois

Customer Service 888-454-2279

Visit our website at www.heinemannlibrary.com

Designed by Ticktock Media and Tim Bones

Originated by Ambassador Litho Ltd.

Printed and Bound in China by South China Printing Company

08 07 06 05 04

10 9 8 7 6 5 4 3 2 1

Library of Congress Cataloging-in-Publication Data

Middleton, Haydn.

Modern Olympics / Haydn Middleton.

p. cm. -- (The Olympics)

Summary: Provides an overview of the modern Olympics that began again in 1896, describing some of the competitive events, looking at how host cities are chosen, profiling various modern Olympic champions, and more. Includes bibliographical references and index.

ISBN 1-4034-4677-6 (Library Binding-hardcover)

1. Olympics--History--Juvenile literature. [1. Olympics--History.] I.

Title. II. Olympics (2003)

GV721.53.M55 2003

796.48--dc21

2003006949

Acknowledgments

The author and publisher are grateful to the following for permission to reproduce copyright material: pp. 4t, 11t, 22r Corbis; p. 5t Ancient Art and Architecture; pp. 4–5b, 6–7, 8–9, 10b, 11b, 12–13, 14–15, 16, 18–19, 20–21, 22t, 23t, 24–25, 26–27 Empics. Cover photographs: Empics

On the cover of this book, several images from the Olympics are shown, including the Olympic torch, an Olympic medal, a baton used in the relay event, and the closing ceremony of the 2000 Olympics in Sydney, Australia. The back cover of this book shows Australia's Cathy Freeman lighting the Olympic flame at the opening ceremony of the 2000 Olympics.

CONTENTS

Some words are shown in bold, **like this.** You can find out what they mean by looking in the glossary.

THE GAMES ARE BACK

Baron Pierre de Coubertin (second from left), father of the modern Olympics, is pictured here with the rest of the first International Olympic Committee, or **IOC.**

In April 1896, a huge sports festival was held in Athens, Greece. It was called the Olympic Games. More than 300 athletes from 14 different countries competed against one another. Huge crowds gathered to watch 43 different events. This 10-day festival took a lot of organizing. The man behind the event was a sports-loving Frenchman named Baron Pierre de Coubertin. People in the world often fought one another in wars, and Coubertin felt they should instead compete in peaceful sports events.

Since 1896, the Olympics have been held in seventeen different countries on four different continents. They remain the most important international athletic competition in the world. In 1997, Athens won the right to bring the Olympics home again to Greece in 2004.

GREAT OLYMPIC EVENTS
Marathon

The longest Olympic foot race is the marathon. Runners have to complete a course that is about 26.2 miles (42.2 kilometers) long. There was no marathon in the ancient Olympics—the longest race then was just 2.87 miles (4,619 meters). According to a legend, the marathon was actually named after a great Greek victory over Persian invaders. A Greek messenger ran all the way from a place called Marathon to Athens— approximately 26 miles (40 kilometers)— with news of the victory, and then dropped dead!

The Olympic Games held in Athens in 1896 were not the first Olympics. The first Olympics were held about 3,000 years ago. For about 1,200 years, athletes from all over the world came to a place called Olympia every four years to compete in a five-day athletics event called the Olympic Games. That was where Coubertin got the idea for the modern Olympics.

This painting on a vase made in ancient Greece shows a chariot race. These races were considered to be the most spectacular events at the ancient Olympic Games.

THEN & NOW
Men only?

*Events at the ancient Olympics included chariot-racing and a race that involved running in armor. Only men were allowed to compete, and married women were not even allowed to watch! The Olympic Games were part of a religious festival held in honor of the Greek god Zeus. The modern Olympics are not religious, and since 1900 women have competed. Women began to compete in **track-and-field** events after 1928.*

WORDS TO REMEMBER

*"The most important thing in the Olympic Games is not to win but to take part, just as the most important thing in life is not the triumph but the struggle." These words, spoken by Baron Pierre de Coubertin, reflect the true spirit of the Olympics. For those who do win, there are no financial rewards, although Olympic champions may receive money through **endorsements** and advertising deals. For many years, only **amateur** athletes were allowed to take part in the Olympics. Today, **professional** athletes can also compete in most Olympic sports.*

Ethiopian Abebe Bikila ran his way to victory in the marathon at the 1960 Olympics in Rome, Italy.

DIFFERENT KINDS OF OLYMPICS

The Jamaican bobsled team competed at the 1998 Winter Olympics in Nagano, Japan.

Since 1896, the Olympics have been held every four years. They have only been canceled three times: in 1916, during World War I, and in 1940 and 1944, during World War II. Since 1924, there have been separate Winter Games and Summer Games. The Summer Olympics include games and events, such as running, tennis, and volleyball. Athletes at the Winter Games compete in events such as skating, skiing, snowboarding, and playing ice hockey. Fewer countries send teams to the Winter Games, because it is not easy to become a great skier or skater in places with warm **climates** and few mountains. However, if you have enough talent, you can take part in the Olympics no matter where you are from. The 1988 Winter Games in Calgary, Canada, for example, first welcomed a four-man bobsled team from the hot island of Jamaica.

WORDS TO REMEMBER

The Olympic motto is made up of three Latin words: citius, altius, and fortius. They mean swifter, higher, and stronger. Each athlete in the Summer Olympics, Winter Olympics, and Paralympic Games aims to perform better than the others. The best-ever Olympic performance in each event is described as an Olympic record.

This photo shows Korea and Peru competing in a volleyball match at the 2000 Games in Sydney, Australia.

GREAT OLYMPIANS

Connie Hansen

At the 1988 Paralympic Games in Seoul, South Korea, Connie Hansen of Denmark won five different Paralympic events. She came in first in the 400-meter, 800-meter, 1,500-meter, and the 5,000-meter races. She also won the wheelchair marathon. At the 1992 Paralympics in Barcelona, Spain, Hansen again won the wheelchair marathon.

Wheelchair athletes competed in the tennis event at the 2000 Paralympics in Sydney, Australia.

Since 1960, there have been Olympic games for athletes with **disabilities.** These games are called the Paralympics. They take place about the same time as the Summer Olympics. The first Paralympics took place in Rome, Italy, in 1960. In 2000, about 4,000 athletes competed at the Paralympics in Sydney, Australia. The Paralympic Winter Games take place about the same time as the Winter Olympics. In yet another kind of Olympics, the Special Olympics, individuals with **mental retardation** participate in Olympic-type events.

THEN & NOW

When are the Winter Games?

At the first Summer Games, there were some winter sports such as figure skating and ice hockey. But in 1924, the first Winter Games were held, in Chamonix, France. The French also held the Summer Olympics in Paris that year. Until 1992, the Winter Games and Summer Games were always held in the same year, although not always in the same country. Since 1994, however, the Winter Games have taken place two years after each Summer Games. The 2002 Winter Games were held in Salt Lake City, Utah, with nearly 2,400 athletes taking part in 78 different events.

SYMBOLS OF THE GAMES

This photo shows the lighting of the Olympic flame at the 2000 Games in Sydney, Australia.

The Olympics today can be watched either in the Olympic stadium of the host country or on television. The games open and close with ceremonies organized by the host country. At the opening of all games, the competitors march in a parade. Athletes from Greece march in front, followed by athletes from all other countries in alphabetical order. In 1928, the organizers of the Olympics started a custom of lighting a flame in the Olympic stadium. Since 1936, this flame has been brought from Olympia, Greece, the place where the Olympics were first held. Before its journey begins, the flame is lit using mirrors to aim the sun's rays and light the flame. Traditionally, athletes carry the flame into the Olympic stadium.

WORDS TO REMEMBER

At the start of each Olympics since 1920, a single athlete takes the Olympic oath on behalf of all the other competitors from around the world. "I promise," he or she says, "that we will take part in these Olympic Games, respecting the rules which govern them, in the true spirit of sportsmanship, for the glory of sport and the honor of our teams."

OLYMPIC MOMENTS

An unforgettable opening

When the 1984 Games were held in Los Angeles, California, the opening ceremony lasted four and a half hours. Hundreds of millions of TV viewers and about 90,000 spectators watched the ceremony. It featured more than 10,000 performers, including a jet-propelled person who flew through the air before landing in the Olympic stadium there, which was named the Coliseum.

A spectacular opening ceremony took place at the 2000 Olympics in Sydney, Australia.

At the closing ceremony the flame is put out, and the five-ringed Olympic flag is taken down. It is then handed over to the city that will host the next Olympics. The flag was designed by Baron de Coubertin and has flown at every Olympics since 1920, when the games were held in Antwerp, Belgium. Back then, the flags of all nations could be made up from the Olympic flag's five colors and white background. Today, the rings stand for the world's five major continents.

Sweden's Lars Froelander (center) won the gold medal in the men's 100-meter butterfly swimming final at the 2000 Games in Sydney, Australia. Australian Michael Klim (left) won the silver, and Australian Geoff Huegill (right) won the bronze.

THE HOST CITY

The city where each Olympics is held is called the host city. The host city for the first modern Olympics, in 1896, was Athens, Greece. More than 100 years later, Athens won the right to host the 28th Olympics in 2004. Sports fans have sometimes asked for every Olympics to be held there, since Greece is the birthplace of the Olympic Games. But because the modern Olympics are now truly **global** festivals, they are staged all over the world.

THEN & NOW
Who pays for the Olympics?

*It costs a lot of money to host the Olympics, and it is becoming more expensive all the time. In 1936, the German government had to pay about $25 million, raised through **taxes,** to stage the Olympics in Berlin. In 1972, when the Olympics were held in Munich, Germany, it cost almost 70 times that amount. The 1976 Games in Montreal, Canada, were so expensive that it took Canadian taxpayers twenty years to cover the cost! Today, **sponsors** help cover the costs. In 1996, companies paid more than $250 million to sponsor the Olympics that took place in Atlanta, Georgia. Money is also raised from making TV companies pay huge sums for the rights to show Olympic events.*

OLYMPIC MOMENTS
Olympic mascots

Since 1972, official mascots have been used as symbols of fun at each Olympic festival. The first mascot was Waldi the Dachshund, a dog who appeared at the 1972 Olympics in Munich, Germany. At the 2000 Games in Sydney, the mascots were based on animals that live in Australia—Millie the echidna, Ollie the kookaburra, and Syd the platypus.

Misha the Russian Bear was the mascot for the 1980 Olympic Games.

SWIFTER, HIGHER, STRONGER . . . FAIRER?

*There is strong competition between cities in different countries to win the right to host the Olympic Games. Bidders from some cities were so eager to win, they cheated. In 1999, a scandal broke out when it was proven that several city officials had given **bribes** to IOC members in return for votes. There was another bribe scandal in the bidding for the 2002 Winter Games. It was alleged that officials from the state of Utah had given gifts to members of the IOC.*

This is a poster from the 1936 Olympic Games, held in Berlin, Germany.

The president of the IOC in 2003 was this man, Jacques Rogge.

The **IOC** decides which city will host the Olympics. To be chosen as a host city is a great honor, so several cities usually put in a **bid.** Eleven cities—including Cape Town, South Africa; Rio de Janeiro, Brazil; and Istanbul, Turkey—put in bids for the 2004 Olympics. The IOC officials choose the city they believe will be the best host to all the athletes and spectators. They make their decision a long time before the Olympics, so that the host city can prepare. In 1993, Sydney was chosen to hold the 27th Olympic Games, which were not due to take place until 2000!

The Olympic Stadium in Athens, Greece, is shown here in 1997.

Each modern Olympics lasts about two weeks. The host city and Olympic officials spend years making sure everything runs smoothly. Because they have to deal with huge numbers of visitors, this is no simple task. For the 1996 Olympics in Atlanta, Georgia, there were eleven million tickets. These spectators could watch different events at 21 **venues** in and around the city. To get them there on time each day, the city's transportation system had to work very efficiently. That is why the organizers called the Atlanta Olympics "the largest peacetime . . . event in human history."

THEN & NOW
How much does safety cost?

At the 1996 Olympics in Atlanta, Georgia, it cost nearly $200 million just to pay for security. Despite this expense, however, one person died and 110 others were injured in a bombing that year at Centennial Olympic Park. Another tragedy in Olympic history took place at the Munich Olympics in Germany in 1972. Terrorists broke into the Olympic Village, and eleven athletes from Israel were killed. A total of 50,000 guards have been hired to patrol the 2004 Olympics in Athens. Greece has received guarantees of security assistance from 37 other countries.

The Olympic flag flew at half-mast to remember those who died at the 1972 Olympics. Today, host countries employ tens of thousands of security guards to try to prevent attacks from happening again.

WORDS TO REMEMBER

*"It takes more than crossing the finish line first to make a champion. A champion . . . rejects **doping.**" These words were spoken by the **IOC** president at the opening of the 2002 Winter Olympics in Salt Lake City, Utah. Athletes must not take illegal drugs that might help them run faster, jump higher, or generally perform better. Since the 1968 Olympics in Mexico City, Mexico, Olympic officials have tested competitors for traces of such drugs. Athletes who fail the test are disqualified and disgraced. The IOC—backed by WADA (the World Anti-Doping Agency)—is determined to ban the use of illegal drugs.*

Canadian sprinter Ben Johnson was caught taking drugs at the 1988 Games in Seoul, South Korea. The gold medal he had won in the 100-meter sprint was taken away, and he was not allowed to compete for several years.

GREAT OLYMPIANS

VOLUNTEERS

The modern Olympics could not take place without volunteer helpers. For no reward except a share in the fun of the Olympics, 46,967 volunteers were busily at work at the 2000 Olympics in Sydney, Australia. More than 60,000 volunteers have signed up to help at the Athens Olympics in 2004. Anyone eighteen years old or older can help, and volunteers come from countries all over the world. The jobs they do include keeping the venues clean, providing food and transportation, and attending to the many needs of athletes, officials, and spectators.

A host city also has to provide accommodations for athletes and officials. During the 1920 Olympics in Antwerp, Belgium, competitors stayed in the city's schools, where eight of them slept in each classroom. At the Los Angeles Olympics in 1932, a new tradition began. A special Olympic Village was built, complete with its own fire station, post office, and hospital. The male athletes stayed in the village. There were only 127 women athletes. They stayed in a Los Angeles hotel. Later, Olympic Villages were built on unused land. When the games are over, local people can then move into the apartments in the village.

OLYMPIC TRACK EVENTS

Wheelchair athlete
Tanni Grey-Thompson has
won nine gold medals in
the Paralympics.

Track events such as the men's 100-meter, 400-meter, and 1,500-meter races have existed since the first modern Olympics in Athens in 1896. Others, such as the 20,000-meter walk, were added later. Some of the best-known Olympians of all time were track athletes. For example, the long-distance runner Emil Zátopek of Czechoslovakia won three gold medals in eight days at the 1952 Olympics in Helsinki, Finland. Sprinter Fanny Blankers-Koen, known as the Dutch Flying Housewife, won four races in the 1948 Olympics in London, England. More recently, at the 1996 Olympics in Atlanta, Georgia, Michael Johnson of the United States became the first man ever to win a gold medal for both the 200-meter and 400-meter races. Four years later, he won the 400-meter race again at the 2000 Olympics in Sydney, Australia.

SWIFTER, HIGHER, STRONGER

This table shows 100-meter sprint records through the years.

Date	Record holder	Time (secs)
1896	Thomas Burke (United States)	12.0
1924	Harold Abrahams (G. Britain)	10.6
1936	Jesse Owens (United States)	10.3
1960	Armin Hary (Germany)	10.2
1964	Robert Hayes (United States)	10.05
1968	James Hines (United States)	9.95
1988	Carl Lewis (United States)	9.92
1996	Donovan Bailey (Canada)	9.84

Distance runner Kipchoge
Keino of Kenya won the
1,500-meter race at the 1968
Olympics in Mexico City, Mexico.

For athletes aiming to break Olympic or world records, timing is key. At the earlier Olympic Games, officials timed runners and walkers with simple stopwatches. Since 1932, however, more accurate electronic timing methods have been used. Instruments called anemometers are used to measure wind speeds for shorter races. If an athlete is going to set an official record, the wind speed behind him or her has to be less than 6.56 feet (2 meters) per second.

OLYMPIC MOMENTS

Cross-country racing

At the Olympics held in 1912, 1920, and 1924, a difficult cross-country race occurred. At the last Olympic cross-country race, held in 1924 in Paris, France, 38 athletes started in the race. Only 15 finished. The course included rocky paths covered in knee-high weeds. There was also a power station nearby that filled the air with toxic fumes. Hours after Paavo Nurmi of Finland won the gold medal, officials were still searching for missing runners by the sides of the road. Since this misfortune, there have been no more Olympic cross-country races.

THEN & NOW

Where are the women?

*Until the 1928 Olympics in Amsterdam, Netherlands, no women were allowed to compete in **track-and-field** events. Some people still believed women's bodies were too delicate for any race longer than 220 yards (200 meters). After the women's 800-meter final in 1928, several runners collapsed. The race was not held again until the 1960 Olympics. The 1,500-meter race for women became a regular Olympic event in 1972, followed in 1984 by the women's marathon.*

Ethiopian runner Derartu Tulu celebrated victory in the 10,000-meter race at the 1992 Olympics in Barcelona, Spain.

Czech Dana Zatopkova won the javelin competition in the 1952 Olympics in Helsinki, Finland.

Like most track events, field events take place inside the Olympic stadium. Field events include throwing competitions such as the javelin, discus, and shot put, as well as jumping events such as the triple jump, pole vault, and long jump. Some, such as the discus, date back to ancient Olympic times. Others have been introduced more recently. The women's pole vault, for example, appeared for the first time at the 2000 Olympics in Sydney, Australia.

*British athlete Daley Thomson won gold medals in the **decathlon** at the 1980 Olympics in Moscow and the 1984 Olympics in Los Angeles.*

GREAT OLYMPIANS

Ray Ewry

More than 100 years before the Paralympics began, American athlete Ray Ewry became ill with a disease called polio. He was told he might never walk again. Ewry, however, exercised on his own, and he not only walked again, but jumped into Olympic history. Between 1900 and 1908, he won a total of eight gold medals in the standing high jump, standing long jump, and standing triple jump. These events were dropped from the Olympics in 1912, but Ewry's magnificent achievements will not be forgotten.

At the triple jump competition in the 1972 Olympics in Munich, the old world record was beaten nine times. The **Soviet Union's** Viktor Saneyev finally won with a gigantic hop, step, and jump of 57.05 feet (17.39 meters). German athlete Ulrike Meyfarth cleared 6.3 feet (1.92 meters) to win the women's high jump. Aged just sixteen, she was the youngest person to have won a gold medal in an Olympic field event. Four years earlier, at the 1968 Olympics in Mexico City, Bob Beamon of the United States made long jump history when he leapt 29.2 feet (8.90 meters), breaking the world record by 22 inches (55 centimeters). The diagram below shows where each field event could take place in an Olympic stadium.

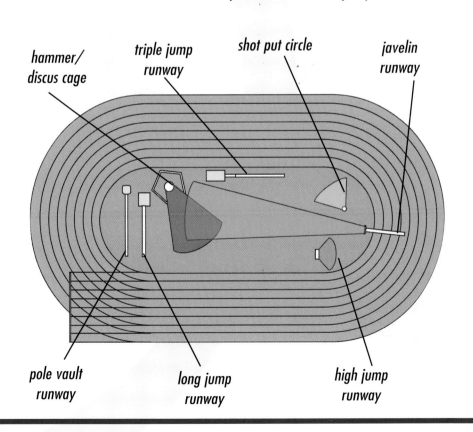

hammer/discus cage

triple jump runway

shot put circle

javelin runway

pole vault runway

long jump runway

high jump runway

OLYMPIC WATER SPORTS

GREAT OLYMPIANS

Wonderkids

Marjorie Gestring of the United States was the youngest individual gold medal winner ever at the Olympics. She won the springboard diving competition at the 1936 Olympics in Berlin, Germany. She was 13 years old. But she may not be the youngest Olympian ever. At the 1900 Olympics in Paris, France, a French boy was chosen to be the person who directed the rowers of a Dutch rowing team. The team won the gold medal. His name is now unknown, and so is his age, but some eyewitnesses thought he may have been as young as seven.

The first Olympic swimming contest was held outdoors, in the icy Bay of Zea at the 1896 Olympics in Athens, Greece. Two of the three races were won by 18-year-old Alfréd Hajós of Hungary. Since then, athletes have continued to compete in front of Olympic crowds from the water— not just swimmers and divers, but canoeists and rowers, too.

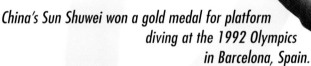

China's Sun Shuwei won a gold medal for platform diving at the 1992 Olympics in Barcelona, Spain.

Australian Dawn Fraser won four gold and four silver medals in Olympic swimming events during the 1960s.

STRANGE BUT TRUE

From the Olympics to the movies

Four Olympic medalists went into the movies to play the role of Tarzan, a popular action hero brought up by apes in the jungle. The most famous swimmer-turned-actor was Johnny Weissmuller. He was born in Romania to German parents, but he swam for the United States after moving there in 1908. The first man to swim the 100-meter race in less than one minute, Johnny won five Olympic gold medals, setting Olympic records in the 100-meter freestyle event in both 1924 and 1928. He was also the star of twelve Tarzan movies!

Denmark's Paul Elvstrom was champion in a **yachting** competition at every Olympics from 1948 to 1960. At the 1972 Olympics in Munich, swimmer Mark Spitz of the United States won seven gold medals— more than anyone else at a single Olympics— and he broke the world record seven times. The **Soviet Union's** Vyacheslav Ivanov rowed to victory in the **single sculls** in 1956, 1960, and 1964. At the 1956 Olympics in Melbourne, Australia, he accidentally dropped his medal in the rowing lake while celebrating his victory, and lost it forever. British rower Steve Redgrave won a record-breaking five consecutive gold medals in Olympic Games held from 1984 until 2000.

Paul Elvstrom of Denmark won four gold medals in different Olympic sailing competitions.

THEN AND NOW

How old?

Great Britain's Thomas Thornycroft won two gold medals for motorboating at the London Olympics in 1908. This sport did not took place again at the Olympics, but Thornycroft appeared again in the Olympic Games 44 years later. He was a member of Great Britain's yachting team at the 1952 games in Helsinki, Finland. He was 70 years old at the time!

OLYMPIC TEAM SPORTS

There were no team sports at the ancient Olympics. Some people believe they do not belong in the modern Olympics either. The Olympics are thought to bring nations together in peace. But when teams from countries unfriendly with one another compete in sports events, it is more likely that arguments will break out. At the 1956 Olympics in Melbourne, Australia, for example, the water polo final between teams from Hungary and the **Soviet Union** turned into a fight and had to be ended early.

GREAT OLYMPIC EVENTS

Hats off to the Hungarians

Soccer has been an Olympic sport since 1900. Women's soccer became an Olympic sport in 1996. At the 1952 Olympics in Helsinki, Finland, Hungary won every one of their Olympic matches, scoring twenty goals, with just two scored against them. In the four years after May 1950, the national team of Hungary did not lose a single soccer game.

OLYMPIC FACTS

The Olympic Games are not competitions between nations. That is one of the **IOC's** rules, and until 1908, all athletes entered the Olympics as individuals. They were not chosen as members of teams from their home countries. But at each Olympics, people in the **media** count up how many medals each national team has won. Then they make a table showing which is the top Olympic country. Only five nations have topped this table: the United States, the Soviet Union, Great Britain, France, and Germany. The all-time winner is the United States.

The Cuban baseball team celebrated with the Cuban flag after beating Japan in the baseball final at the 1996 Olympics in Atlanta, Georgia.

In sledge hockey, players move themselves around on the ice on specially made sleds with skate blades attached to the bottom. This image is from a sledge hockey match at the 2002 Paralympic Winter Games.

At the 1972 Olympics in Munich, the Russians scored in the last second of the basketball final to beat the United States by 51 points to 50. Arguments broke out after the game because more time had been put back on the clock by the referee after the game had officially ended. In another contest in 1972, **West Germany** won the men's field hockey final against Pakistan. The Pakistanis threw water on an official and refused to face the West German flag when the West German national anthem was played.

STRANGE BUT TRUE

The first modern Olympians

Some of the athletes who competed in the first modern Olympics in Athens, Greece, were tourists that just happened to be in the area in 1896. The athletes were not chosen by their countries to compete in the Olympics. Instead, they came individually and had to pay their own expenses. Cycling, gymnastics, swimming, target shooting, tennis, and weight lifting were all events at the first modern Olympics.

This picture shows a scene from a men's water polo game at the 2000 Olympics in Sydney, Australia.

OLYMPIC GYMNASTICS

A rhythmic gymnast demonstrates her skills.

Gymnastics were very popular in ancient Greece. They became popular again during the 1700s in Germany, where most of the **apparatus** for modern gymnastics was invented. Men have competed at Olympic gymnastics events ever since the 1896 Olympics in Athens. Since 1900, each Olympics has had an overall gymnastics champion. This is the athlete with the best total score in several different exercises. These now include floor exercises and routines on the horizontal and parallel bars. A team event for women gymnasts was introduced at the 1928 Olympics in Amsterdam, Netherlands. Then, at the Olympic Games in Helsinki, Finland, in 1952, women started to compete as individuals.

The Romanian gymnast Nadia Comaneci won three gold medals in Montreal, Canada in 1976.

GREAT OLYMPIANS

Olga Korbut

At the 1972 Olympics in Munich, many people enjoyed watching the gymnast Olga Korbut of the **Soviet Union,** even though she came in seventh place overall. She was seventeen years old, 4.9 feet (150 centimeters) tall, and weighed just 86 pounds (39 kilograms). Tiny Olga stood out for her smile and sense of fun, which won her millions of fans who watched her on television. She went on to win gold medals for her floor and balance-beam exercises.

In order to become an Olympic champion, a gymnast must score the most points for his or her performances, which are judged by an international panel. It is made up of six judges who watch the gymnast's every move in detail. The highest possible starting score is ten. Points, or fractions of a point, are then taken away each time the gymnast makes a mistake.

Sawao Kato of Japan is shown here on the parallel bars at the 1976 Olympics in Montreal, Canada.

OLYMPIC FACTS

Perfect ten

Until the 1976 Olympics in Montreal, Canada, no gymnast had ever scored a perfect ten out of ten. Then, a fourteen-year-old gymnast from Romania named Nadia Comaneci achieved this feat no fewer than seven times. Her closest rival for first place, Nelli Kim of the Soviet Union, scored a ten twice, too. The electronic scoreboard could not cope. The highest score it was able to show was 9.95—so it just flashed 1.00! Soon after those Olympics, eight-year-old Mary Lou Retton of the United States scored a 1.00 in her first competition. Thinking it was meant to be a 10.00, she jumped for joy. But this time the scoreboard was correct— she really had scored just 1.00. Mary Lou Retton kept training and at the 1984 Olympics in Los Angeles, she scored some real perfect tens to win an Olympic gold medal.

GREAT OLYMPIC EVENTS

Women's Team Gymnastics from the Soviet Union

After the end of World War II in 1945, gymnastics became a top sport in Eastern Europe. No country produced more champion gymnasts than the Soviet Union. In each of the ten Olympics that it entered from 1952 until 1996, a Soviet women's team won the gold medal for the combined exercises. In the same period, a Soviet men's team won gold medals five times.

OLYMPIC POWER AND PRECISION

Iran's Hossein Rezazadeh won a gold medal in weight lifting at the 2000 Olympics in Sydney, Australia.

Many of the world's strongest athletes compete in Olympic sports such as boxing, fencing, judo, and wrestling. Some have won even greater fame after the Olympics. Muhammad Ali, Teófilo Stevenson, and Evander Holyfield all went on to become **professional** boxing champions. The weight lifter Harold Sakata became an international movie star in the 1964 James Bond movie *Goldfinger*.

The boxer Cassius Clay, who later changed his name to Muhammad Ali, won the light heavyweight crown at the 1960 Olympics in Rome, Italy.

STRANGE BUT TRUE

Winning by weight

At the 1956 Olympics in Melbourne, Australia, two weight lifters tied for first place in the superheavyweight event. Both Humberto Selvetti of Argentina and Paul Anderson of the United States lifted a total of just more than 1,100 pounds (500 kilograms). This gave them a new Olympic record to share, but who was to get the gold medal? The answer was Anderson, because his own body weight was 12.35 pounds (5.6 kilograms) less than Selvetti's. To get into shape for the Olympics, Anderson had lost more than 55 pounds (25 kilograms)!

WORDS TO REMEMBER

Boris "Dis-Onishenko"

*At the 1976 Olympics in Montreal, Canada, sports experts thought the **Soviet Union** team would win the modern pentathlon. But the team was disqualified when team member Boris Onishenko was found cheating in fencing. Fencers wear sensors so that when a sword tip touches an opponent to score a hit, a light goes on. Onishenko had fixed his sword so that he could make the light come on just by pressing a button. For this piece of dishonesty, the **media** quickly gave him a new name: "Dis-Onishenko."*

The Olympic motto is "Swifter, Higher, Stronger." "Accurate" would best describe the **precision** sports of archery, fencing, shooting, and horse riding—the only sport in which men and women still compete against each other. Competitors in the five events of the modern **pentathlon** have to be precise and powerful. This sport is based on the idea of a soldier delivering a message. It includes riding, fencing, shooting, swimming, and cross-country running.

SWIFTER, HIGHER, STRONGER

Chris Boardman's super cycle

*Power and precision came together at the 1992 Olympics in Barcelona, Spain. That was when Great Britain's Chris Boardman showed the world his startling new bicycle. Specially built by the Lotus Engineering Company, it weighed only about twenty pounds (nine kilograms). With its one-piece **aerodynamic** frame and three-spoke front wheel, it looked like something from a science-fiction movie! Boardman broke the world record on it twice before his final race, then easily won the gold medal. Some said anyone could have won on the bike, but Jens Lehmann, the German silver medalist, said that he was beaten by the man, not the machine.*

Chris Boardman rode a new kind of bicycle at the 1992 Olympics in Barcelona, Spain.

TRUE OLYMPIC SPIRIT

Since 1896, there have been 27 scheduled Summer Olympics. Athens 2004 is the 28th. There have also been 19 Winter Olympics and 11 Paralympics. Tens of thousands of athletes have competed for Olympic gold medals, but the modern Olympics are not all about winning. Part of the Olympic Creed reads, "The most important thing in the Olympics is not to win but to take part." A creed is a set of guiding rules or beliefs. Every athlete is expected to take this creed very seriously.

Boxing legend Muhammad Ali lit the Olympic flame at the 1996 Olympics in Atlanta, Georgia.

WORDS TO REMEMBER

"Thanks, King"

At the 1912 Olympics in Stockholm, Sweden, the same athlete won the gold medal in both the **pentathlon** and the **decathlon.** This exciting athlete was Jim Thorpe of the United States, who was part Native American, part French, and part Irish. King Gustav V of Sweden said to him, "Sir, you are the greatest athlete in the world." The shy Thorpe replied, "Thanks, King."

SWIFTER, HIGHER, STRONGER . . . KINDER

The winner of the 6.25-mile (10-kilometer) cross-country skiing gold medal at the 1992 Winter Olympics in Albertville, France, was Vegard Ulvang of Norway. The event took place during heavy snowfall. Ulvang's coaches advised him to wax his skis to cope with the conditions. But another competitor, Ebbe Hartz of Denmark, told him it would be better not to do this. Ulvang took Hartz's advice and went on to beat him!

Luz Long showed the Olympic spirit in the 1936 Olympics. The games that year were held in Berlin, Germany, Luz Long's homeland. Germany's rulers, led by Adolf Hitler, claimed that its athletes were superior to all others, especially blacks. In the long jump, Long had to compete against the African American Jesse Owens. Long, who hated **racism,** gave Owens a hint on how to improve his form. Owens went on to win the gold medal. Long himself won the silver medal, and he had gained a new friend for the rest of his life. Like so many of the other men and women featured in this book, Luz Long was not just a great athlete. He was a great Olympian.

Luz Long (left) and Jesse Owens (right) competed against one another in the 1936 Olympics.

GREAT OLYMPIANS

The Flying Finn

Between 1912 and 1936, track athletes from Finland won 24 gold medals. Nine of them were won by Paavo Nurmi, a long-distance runner who set 29 world records between 1920 and 1928. In 1952, the Olympics were held in Helsinki, Finland. At the opening ceremony, a runner entered the Olympic stadium carrying the torch. The many Finnish people in the crowd recognized his famous running style and broke into thunderous clapping. It was the great Flying Finn, Paavo Nurmi, who was 55 years old at the time.

*Cathy Freeman, an **Aboriginal**-Australian, won the gold medal in the 400-meter race at the 2000 Olympics in Sydney.*

OLYMPIC TIME LINES AND FACTS

This table shows where the Summer Games have been held. It also shows how many athletes participated and the number of Olympic events.

YEAR/HOST COUNTRY	MALE COMPETITORS	FEMALE COMPETITORS	NATIONS PARTICIPATING	NUMBER OF EVENTS
1896 Athens, Greece	311	0	14	43
1900 Paris, France	1,206	19	26	87
1904 St. Louis, Missouri, U.S.	681	6	13	94
1908 London, England	1,999	36	22	109
1912 Stockholm, Sweden	2,490	57	28	102
1916 Games Cancelled During World War I				
1920 Antwerp, Belgium	2,591	78	29	154
1924 Paris, France	2,956	136	44	126
1928 Amsterdam, Netherlands	2,724	290	46	109
1932 Los Angeles, California, U.S.	1,281	27	37	116
1936 Berlin, Germany	3,738	328	49	129
1940 Games Cancelled During World War II				
1944 Games Cancelled During World War II				
1948 London, England	3,714	385	59	136
1952 Helsinki, Finland	4,407	518	69	149
1956 Melbourne, Australia	2,958	384	72	151
1960 Rome, Italy	4,738	610	83	50
1964 Tokyo, Japan	4,457	683	93	163
1968 Mexico City, Mexico	4,750	781	112	172
1972 Munich, West Germany	6,065	1,058	121	195
1976 Montreal, Canada	4,781	1,247	92	198
1980 Moscow, Soviet Union	4,092	125	80	203
1984 Los Angeles, California, U.S.	5,230	1,567	140	221
1988 Seoul, South Korea	6,279	2,186	159	237
1992 Barcelona, Spain	6,659	2,708	169	257
1996 Atlanta, Georgia, U.S.	6,797	3,513	197	271
2000 Sydney, Australia	6,582	4,069	199	300
2004 Athens, Greece	about 6,600	about 5,980	about 199	301

OLYMPIC FACTS AND FIGURES

How good were ancient Olympians compared to modern ones? Records survive of Protesilaus, an ancient Greek who threw the discus 151 feet (46 meters). Robert Garrett of the United States won the event at the 1896 Olympics in Athens with a throw of 95.6 feet (29.14 meters). At the 1988 Olympics in Seoul, South Korea, Jurgen Schult of Germany won the gold medal with a throw of 225.79 feet (68.82 meters).

*Who won the most Olympic medals? Gymnast Larisa Latynina (**Soviet Union**) won eighteen medals between 1956 and 1964.*

Who was the oldest Olympic medalist? Oscar Swahn of Sweden's shooting team competed at the age of 72 at the 1920 Olympics in Antwerp, Belgium.

Which country has had the longest winning streak in a single Olympic event? Athletes from the United States won the pole vault at every Olympics from 1896 to 1968.

What is the longest time between winning performances by the same athlete? Hungarian fencer Aladár Gerevich won Olympic gold in 1932 and then again in 1960, with a a gap of 28 years between medals.

WINTER GAMES TIME LINE

This table shows the year and city of each Winter Olympics.

1924 CHAMONIX, FRANCE

1928 ST. MORITZ, SWITZERLAND

1932 LAKE PLACID, NEW YORK, U.S.

1936 GARMISCH-PARTENKIRCHEN, GERMANY

1948 ST. MORITZ, SWITZERLAND

1952 OSLO, NORWAY

1956 CORTINA, ITALY

1960 SQUAW VALLEY, CALIFORNIA, U.S.

1964 INNSBRUCK, AUSTRIA

1968 GRENOBLE, FRANCE

1972 SAPPORO, JAPAN

1976 INNSBRUCK, AUSTRIA

1980 LAKE PLACID, NEW YORK, U.S.

1984 SARAJEVO, YUGOSLAVIA

1988 CALGARY, ALBERTA, CANADA

1992 ALBERTVILLE, FRANCE

1994 LILLEHAMMER, NORWAY

1998 NAGANO, JAPAN

2002 SALT LAKE CITY, UTAH, U.S.

2006 TURIN, ITALY

GLOSSARY

aboriginal *having to do with the original people who live in a region*

aerodynamic *of or related to something designed to reduce wind resistance*

aluminum *lightweight but very strong metal*

amateur *person who plays sports or does activities for pleasure rather than pay*

apparatus *equipment used to perform on in gymnastic events*

bid *process by which a country registers its interest to host an Olympics*

bribe *money or favor given or promised in order to influence a person*

climate *weather conditions that are usual for a certain area*

decathlon *athletic contest usually limited to men in which each contestant participates in the following ten track-and-field events: the 100-meter, 400-meter, and 1,500-meter runs; the 110-meter high hurdles; the discus and javelin throws; the shot put; the pole vault; and the high jump and long jump.*

disabled *physically or mentally unable to do something or make a certain action*

doping *when an athlete uses drugs to improve his or her performance*

fiberglass *strong, lightweight material made up of glass fibers*

freestyle *swimming event or leg of an event in which the contestants may use any stroke*

global *something popular or known all over the world*

IOC *International Olympic Committee, the group in charge of organizing the Olympics*

media *journalists from newspapers, TV stations, and other organizations that publish news*

mental retardation *condition in which a person's mental and everyday functioning are seriously impaired or damaged*

pentathlon *athletic contest in which each competitor competes in five track-and-field events, the 200-meter and 1,500-meter runs, the long jump, and the discus and javelin throws*

precision *term used to refer to a sport that requires a great deal of accuracy*

professional *somebody who earns a living competing in a sport or doing an activity*

racism *when someone bases an opinion of someone else on the person's color or race*

single scull *very small, light racing boat*

Soviet Union *former communist country that included Russia and fourteen other republics. It officially was broken up on December 31, 1991.*

sponsor *person or organization that gives money to an organization or plans an event*

tax *money paid to the government by businesses or people for public use*

track-and-field *relating to sports events that usually take place inside an oval running track. Track events take place on a running track. Field events include throwing and jumping competitions.*

venue *location where events or meetings are held*

West Germany *name for the Republic of Germany. From 1949 to 1990, Germany was divided into two republics popularly known as East Germany and West Germany.*

wreath *band of flowers or leaves shaped into a ring*

MORE BOOKS TO READ

Ditchfield, Christin. *Top 10 American Women's Olympic Gold Medalists.* Berkeley Heights, N.J.: Enslow Publishers, 2000.

Kennedy, Mike. *Special Olympics.* Danbury, Conn.: Scholastic Library, 2003.

Middleton, Haydn. *Crises at the Olympics.* Chicago: Heinemann Library, 1999.

Middleton, Haydn. *Great Olympic Moments.* Chicago: Heinemann Library, 1999.

Middleton, Haydn. *Modern Olympic Games.* Chicago: Heinemann Library, 1999.

INDEX